Fuel Your Future:
Power Up for the World of Work

Fuel Your Future:
Power Up for the World of Work

Dr. Keisha Stephenson Taylor

Copyright © 2025 Keisha Stephenson Taylor

Published by Keisha Stephenson Taylor

ISBN: 979-8-218-67344-4

All rights reserved. No part of this book may be reproduced or transmitted in any form or by any means, electronic or mechanical, including photocopying and recording, or by an information storage and retrieval system, without prior written permission from the author.

Dedication

This book is a tribute to the many incredible people who have supported, encouraged, and inspired me along the way. To my family, whose love and unwavering belief in me truly buoys me, Marc, Carter, Corbin, thank you; you told me that I could, and made me believe.

To my parents, Joseph and Yvonne Stephenson, sisters, nieces, nephews, aunts, uncles, and cousins; our shared history, rich Jamaican heritage, and culture have been my foundation, and I am truly blessed to have you cheering me on.

To my beloved friends who I lovingly call "Framily", who console, nurture, and lift me up when I feel weary, I cannot think of a more incredible group who I adore and cherish.

To my mentors and colleagues, who have challenged me to think bigger, do more, and be proud of the impact I make, I thank you for taking my early and late calls and texts from me, and supporting me through every step of this journey.

I want to thank all of you for the guidance, wisdom, and kindness that have shaped not only this work but also the person I am today. I am deeply grateful for each of you.

Finally, to the readers, this book serves as a guide, a source of encouragement, and a reminder that you are more than capable of achieving success in the world of work. This is your journey, and I am honored to be a small part of it.

With heartfelt gratitude,
Dr. Keisha Stephenson Taylor

Testimonials

"Fuel Your Future: Power Up for the World of Work is a game-changer for anyone transitioning from school to the workforce. Dr. Taylor has been a constant guide in my professional journey from when I was a high school intern to a full-time professional and MBA candidate. Her guidance has not only helped me navigate the uncertainties of early career steps but has also empowered me to make confident and strategic decisions. Her practical advice and real-world insights have been instrumental in my own career growth, and I am so excited to see the knowledge in this book impact the next generation of leaders." ~ Katherine Aycock, Oklahoma State University, Class of 2020

This book feels like having a mentor just a phone call away. It's full of honest advice, helpful tips, and the kind of encouragement you need when stepping into the working world. Whether you're just graduating or making a career move, it gives you the confidence to move forward. ~ Elizabeth Rivera, Licensed Custom Trades and Operations Agent

Dr. Taylor is an inspiring colleague whose passion for student success is evident in everything she does. I have seen her, live in action, speak at our institution's Leadership Development Day where she spoke about Professionalism and Self-Development. She invited the students to reflect and implement action steps throughout the presentation. Her guidance has had a lasting impact on my own career journey, as she leads by example as both a mentor and a role model. This book is a must-read for anyone navigating college, career, or career transition—it captures her wisdom and commitment to helping others thrive. ~ Meredith Brown, CCSP Career Advisor, Rowan College Burlington County, NJ

This book is a powerful and timely resource for anyone stepping into the workforce or navigating a career transition. As someone in the early stages of my career, the insights and tools shared by Dr. Keisha Taylor reflect the exact kind of support that helped me build confidence and find direction. It highlights the importance of mentorship and connection, things that made all the difference for me. It's a must-read for future professionals who understand that career success begins with community. ~ Madison McDaniel, Stockton University 2023

When I was searching for a position after graduation, Dr. Keisha emphasized the importance of expanding my network and engaging in conversations with professionals in my desired industry. These conversations not only gave me valuable insight into the industry from different perspectives but also helped me become more confident and comfortable speaking with professionals—ultimately improving my interview skills. Building my network also introduced me to opportunities I wouldn't have discovered by simply applying for roles online. ~ Savana LaRocca University of Maryland 2024

In Hight School, the guidance department is prepared to help students going to college or into the service. If this is not your path, you are basically left to figure it out for yourself. Luckily, we know Dr. Keisha Taylor, who helped me solidify my goals and then connected me to union representatives who guided me in the right direction. This saved me countless hours as well as money that I would have spent had I gone an alternative route. Everyone should be fortunate enough to have a Dr. Keisha Taylor in their corner! ~ Grant Turgeon, 2022 High School Graduate

Dr. Keisha Stephenson Taylor helped me navigate systems that are not always welcoming. She taught me the unspoken secrets of succeeding as a corporate woman—a privilege, not everyone has the chance to get passed down. Attending a historically black college built my confidence but working with Dr. Keisha taught me how to use that confidence to enter spaces as a force. By bridging my HBCU experiences with the corporate world, she showed me how to make my voice heard, and my presence felt in spaces that weren't built for someone like me. This book is a must-read for anyone looking to break through barriers and make their mark. ~ Kaya Strother Spelman College Class of 2024

I have seen Dr. Keisha's wisdom in action as a speaker, collaborator, and personal supporter of my career development. This book will provide you with tangible action steps and transformative insight to step confidently into your next professional role. If you are like me and just hearing the words "job search"; "resume"; and "networking" is enough to cause feelings of nervousness, fear not! You are in the right place and in good hands with this book. ~ Alexys Anderson, Rowan College, Burlington County, NJ

Whether it was professional or personal, my niece Keisha has shared ideas, goals to consider and daily counseling over coffee on the phone. Her insights are always uplifting, realistic and honest. When I thought it was near time to retire, we discussed what that would look like. Before the end of the conversation, I had to pivot, be more strategic and become the planner that she thought I could be. The tables have turned in life as I am sure happens often. Every day is better because of our morning coffee, her sharing positive experiences and I get the benefit of her love, guidance and support. ~ Sharon Stephenson-Rojan

Dr. Taylor played a pivotal role in my career transition by helping me sharpen my resume and identify key resources aligned with my goals. Her personalized guidance gave me the clarity and confidence I needed to take the next step professionally. The insight and support she provides are not only practical but truly empowering! If the book is half as insightful as the information she's provided me over the years, it will truly be game-changing for anyone navigating a new chapter in their career journey. ~ Kenneth Strother III, University of Delaware, class of 2021

There are so many nuances in the 'school to workforce' transition for students. This book fills in those gaps, acting as a guide for new and young professionals to have the confidence to move into and throughout the workplace. This book needs to be on every young professional's bookshelf! ~ Dr. Maurice A. Mathis, Senior Director, Pre-College Programs

Table of Contents

Dedication 5

Testimonials 6

About the Author 10

Foreword 12

Introduction 14

Chapter 1 Charging Up: Essential Power Skills for the Job Market 16

Chapter 2 Your Digital DNA: Building a Career-Ready Online Presence 32

Chapter 3 Refining Your Career Identity: Craft a Personal Brand and Statement 42

Chapter 4 Uncover Your Why: Aligning Your Passion, Interests, and Purpose in Your Career 52

Chapter 5 Impact Beyond the Workplace: Building Career Success Through Community Engagement 64

Chapter 6 Stepping Into Opportunity – Maximizing Career Fairs for Success 73

Chapter 7 Purpose Evolution – Building the Skills that Build Your Future 81

Chapter 8 Staying on Track: Building a Career That Grows with You 90

Career Prep Checklist 105

About the Author

Dr. Keisha Stephenson Taylor is a dedicated leader in education, career readiness and workforce development, dedicated to preparing young adults for the evolving demands of the workplace. With a passion for bridging the gap between education and employment, she ensures that young professionals have the skills, knowledge, and connections needed to succeed in the competitive job market.

Keisha's work over the years equips students and alumni with critical workplace skills, where she emphasizes the importance of professionalism, versatility, problem-solving, and adaptability. She develops career readiness programs, helping young professionals build essential skills to search for and prepare for a role. Her one-on-one sessions with young emerging professionals focus on resume writing, interviewing, networking, and understanding workplace culture. Through her many collaborations with workforce development coalitions, Keisha has a unique perspective of what employers are looking for in creating career pathways, supporting internship to hire pipelines, and mentoring programs. She encourages emerging professionals to gain real world experience and industry exposure that support direct hiring opportunities.

Dr. Taylor supports the community through extensive board service, serving on boards where she is passionate about the mission and vision, sharing her commitment to supporting and improving the lives of others.

Keisha holds a bachelor's and master's degree from Rowan University and earned her Doctorate in Educational Leadership and Innovation from Wilmington University. She is a proud mother of two college-age sons and enjoys traveling and learning to play golf with her husband.

Contact Dr. Keisha Stephenson Taylor below!

Foreword

Career and Technical Education has a disappointing history in the United States. In the not-too-distant past, career education was seen as an alternative pathway for those students with lesser abilities than the students who were planning to go to college. It was seen as workforce training for students to take on menial jobs in an economy that no longer exists.

Manufacturing has changed dramatically. Non-thinking assembly line positions are diminishing rapidly. With the advent of AI, workplaces will be changing at an even more rapid pace. The skills now required in our advanced economy are more about problem recognition and problem solving. In order to be successful in the current and future working environment students need to be able to plot a pathway that cultivates their ability to work with and to provide leadership to a team.

In this book, Dr. Taylor lays out strategies for educators and students to take advantage of a current career desire to engage students in learning and personal development that goes beyond an individual career plan. More importantly, she also explains how the career pathway could and should be seen as a catalyst for student growth. She uses her deep knowledge of the challenges students face in their personal development. She does this by relating narratives from students she has had the opportunity to engage with as a caring mentor. Thus, helping them to envision possibilities that more closely align with their aspirations rather than merely settling for gaining employment.

Using this book as a guide will have a significant impact on individual educators and students as they grow as individuals. Students will thrive as their aspirations are identified and followed. They will come to see their education as much more than career development. They will be prepared to act with confidence as they embrace an understanding of their own empowerment to embrace their future.

In *Fuel Your Future: Power Up for the World of Work,* Dr. Taylor has created a wonderful guidebook that should be in everyone's library.

Joseph DiMartino
Brown University Faculty Club Board of Advisors

Introduction

The transition from school to the workforce is a journey filled with excitement, uncertainty, and countless lessons. As young professionals step into the world of work, they often grapple with questions about career paths, networking, confidence, and navigating professional spaces. This book is designed to be a guide—offering insights, strategies, and real-world wisdom to help individuals not only secure opportunities but thrive in them.

Throughout my career, I have had the privilege of mentoring countless individuals, supporting them as they carve out their unique paths. The stories of my mentees, shared in this book, highlight the power of mentorship, community, and strategic preparation. These young professionals, like many others, faced doubts, challenges, and moments of hesitation. However, through guidance, encouragement, and the right connections, they found clarity, confidence, and success in their respective fields.

One mentee shared how our conversations provided not just career advice but a sense of empowerment—encouraging her to step beyond self-doubt and apply for opportunities she might have otherwise overlooked. Another mentee, in just a short time, found a strong network of professionals who opened doors she had never imagined possible. Each testimonial underscores an essential truth: no one succeeds alone.

As you turn the pages of this book, you will discover practical steps to prepare for the workforce, build a network, present yourself confidently, and embrace opportunities with self-assurance.

Success is not merely about landing a job, it is about growing, learning, and finding fulfillment in your career. *Fuel Your Future: Power Up for the World of Work* is your companion on that journey, offering you tools and inspiration to take those next steps with confidence. Whether you are a recent graduate, an early-career professional, or someone looking to pivot into a new opportunity, my hope is that you walk away feeling empowered, prepared, and ready to embrace your future.

Welcome to a journey of preparation, empowerment, and success in the world of work.

Chapter 1
Charging Up: Essential Power Skills for the Job Market

Tyla's Journey to Workplace Readiness

Tyla is a hardworking college student, eager to make a difference. As a business administration major, she envisioned herself leading teams and working in corporate strategy. When she landed her first internship interview at a marketing agency, she was excited—but also nervous.

During the interview, the hiring manager asked, "Can you tell me about a time you worked on a team project and resolved a challenge?"

Tyla froze. She had done plenty of group projects in class, but she struggled to put her experiences into words. She mumbled something about working well with others, but she could tell the answer lacked impact. The interviewer smiled kindly but moved on.

Afterward, Tyla reflected on what went wrong. She realized she hadn't practiced articulating her experiences in a way that showcased her skills. While she had strong teamwork and problem-solving abilities, she hadn't learned how to communicate effectively—a crucial skill for any job.

Congratulations on deciding to accelerate your career preparation for a rapidly changing workplace! Thinking about a career can be connected to your educational pathway, work-related experience, or both. Let's begin with what employers seek and the talent they seek in the job market. In my years of working with students from middle school through graduate level, there have been several skills that I have expressed to my students as being critical or essential in developing a positive workplace environment – power skills. Power skills are interpersonal and behavioral competencies that enable employees to collaborate effectively and adapt to challenges. Technical skills are important, but power skills are essential for long-term success in the workplace.

Employers often regard these essential skills as determining factors when interviewing and assessing candidates. These skills are critical for job success across roles in any organization, regardless of industry or role. Employers have shared with me that they value the power skills they see in candidates and new employees because the stronger these skills are from the start, the more employers will be able to connect these skills to aspiring leaders in their company and organization.

Because these skills and behaviors are taught over time, they are harder to instill and require personal growth and self-awareness; during interviews, it is important to share your experience using and highlighting these skills so that hiring committee members can see the skills you possess on full display. Essentially, they can witness live and in real time the exact power skills they are looking for in their company leadership.

Companies and organizations are focused on organizational performance that supports their goals and outcomes. Employees with strong collaboration and communication skills are essential and help to increase performance and reduce inefficiencies. Early career individuals need to convey these skills throughout the company and organization. There is a demand for creativity, critical thinking, and adaptability in the workplace, and has become increasingly important in the changing workplace and the increased use of automation for initial tasks. Let's dig into these essential skills needed in the workplace!

- ❖ Communication: the ultimate career superpower
- ❖ Collaboration: working well with others
- ❖ Problem-Solving: adapting and thinking on your feet
- ❖ Emotional Intelligence (EQ): your hidden career secret sauce
- ❖ Time Management: getting more accomplished without burnout
- ❖ Resilience and Grit: pushing through challenges

They are all different, but ultimately these skills are what the employers want to see in their prospective employees. A way to think through highlighting these skills is by sharing evidence and examples in your conversations with potential employers or to those around you in your network. In any marketplace, you must be able to have a clear articulation of ideas you would like to express. See the list below with additional information and examples for each of these essential skills:

Communication:

Communication is the clear articulation of ideas, active listening, and message adaptation for various audiences. It is a clear and confident exchange that, when mastered, can prove to be extremely effective in your career. Mastering communication means you have gained the Ability to articulate ideas clearly, both verbally and in writing. This includes listening actively and tailoring messages to diverse audiences.

Communication has several elements that are each important in their own right and are skills that should not only be understood but also developed.

- **Active listening:** being an active listener requires practice, and it displays a level of empathy towards the other person. As you read through this section, you will want to think about a few of the strategies below to think about how to become an active listener.
    - **Paraphrasing:** repeat what you heard in the directions or instructions to gain understanding and clarity.
    - **Asking Clarifying Questions:** ask probing questions to sift and sort out the exact challenge or issue.
    - **Summarizing:** hear and restate in condensed format what you recently heard or observed, again showing that you are present in the conversation.
        - If someone says, "We're struggling to meet this deadline," you could respond with, "It sounds like the timeline is tight. How can I help?"
    - **Using Verbal Acknowledgments:** express what you heard by using language of support or expressions of disagreement.

- Reflecting Feelings: share a common feeling or expression that is observed, sympathizing within the conversation.
- Maintaining Eye Contact: physically demonstrate attentiveness by maintaining steady but natural eye contact with the speaker.
- Avoiding Interruptions: allow the speaker to finish their thoughts before you respond; showing respect and giving them space to fully express themselves.
- Using Nonverbal Cues: provide gestures like head nodding, leaning slightly forward, and using an open posture to convey engagement.
  - Did you know 55% of communication is body language? It's not just about what you say—it's how you say it."
- Offering Solutions Only When Asked: offer suggestions when asked, waiting for the speaker to create space for this offer of support.

- **Message adaptation:** this is another vital skill because you will likely have a different audience than your peers or members of your community. This requires practice and the more you do it, the better you will become at adjusting your messages. Message adaptation involves tailoring communication to suit a specific audience, purpose, or context. Here are a few examples of

when you may have to adapt your message in the workplace.
- **Professional Email:** emails are written documentation, so they should reflect the audience to whom you are writing. Emails should maintain and convey professionalism throughout your message.
- **Social Invitations:** socializing with coworkers is a part of most jobs and careers. The way forward with these interactions is to be sure to maintain a level of professionalism as you reach out to your colleagues, the message you want to convey at all times, even in the social context is that you can message clearly to your colleagues.

Collaboration:

Collaboration is the act of working together with others to achieve a shared goal. Companies don't just want to know what you can do, they want to know what you can do with others. They want to see your ability to work in diverse groups, resolve conflicts, and create collectively. No matter the industry, teamwork is **non-negotiable.** And one thing I know to be true is that great collaborators know how to listen, contribute, and resolve conflicts professionally.

Collaboration consists of these 3 keys:

- **Strong teamwork**
  - Teamwork and the ability to work in diverse groups.

- **Effective conflict resolution**
    - **Conflict Resolution**: as conflicts arise, it is important to focus on the issue and not the individual. Focus on how to get back on task or project timeline and remove any message of blame, but a message of resolution.
- **Thriving in diverse group settings**
    - Every team has its own dynamic. Some people are natural leaders, others are the idea generators, and some are the doers. Understanding your role within the team can help you contribute effectively.
        - Identify the team's goals and how your skills align with them.
        - Be adaptable—sometimes you'll lead, and sometimes you'll support.
        - Respect everyone's contributions, even if they work differently from you.
- Here are a few examples below:
    - **Team Projects**: Employees from different departments working together to develop a new product or service.
    - **Brainstorming Sessions**: A team and design team with different opinions collaborating to create an innovative project.
    - **Cross-functional Teams**: Two internal teams to join forces to implement a new system.

Problem-Solving:

Problem-Solving involves analytical thinking to address challenges and propose innovative solutions. It is a skill that must be continually developed and requires adaptability in dynamic environments. Problem-solving also requires maintaining focus and perseverance in the face of setbacks. Employers want people who can **solve problems, not just identify them.** Candidates who use analytical and innovative approaches to challenges, with adaptability to dynamic environments.

- **Adaptability:** being adaptable means staying flexible, open to feedback, and embracing change.
- In problem-solving, use this framework: IDEA
    o Identify – what and where is the problem that needs solving
    o Define – give the problem a meaning and purpose
    o Explore solutions – Brainstorm and exhaust all possible answers
    o Act – execute the best answer to your problem

Here are a few examples below:

- Workplace: a team presents an issue with deadlines that have been consistently missed. A meeting is held to understand the gaps in communication and the existing process. A new tool is introduced to help with tracking and staying aligned with dates. Resulting in tasks

being tracked effectively, and deadlines being met consistently
- Conflict Resolution: two employees are in conflict, and it is impacting team dynamics. A conversation is facilitated to have both employees share their issue and insight. In the meeting, you should establish common goals and language and develop a resolution plan. This results in team regaining team productivity.

Emotional Intelligence (EQ):

High EQ professionals manage emotions, navigate workplace dynamics, and handle criticism well. They display a great sense of emotional awareness and empathy which improves relationships and fosters teamwork. Individuals with a high emotional intelligence pause and ask themselves, *"What's the best response for this situation?"*

EQ is a critical skill in the workplace as it enhances communication, teamwork, leadership, problem-solving, and overall professional success. Employees with high emotional intelligence are more likely to get promoted, they demonstrate trustworthiness and they strengthen collaboration. Emotionally intelligent leaders manage their own emotions and inspire their teams to stay motivated.

This is one of the essential workplace readiness skills that employers look for in an employee. Here are a few examples below of what makes up emotional intelligence.

- **Self-Awareness:**

- o Recognize when you are stressed or need a break to adjust your approach and reduce the opportunity to be impulsive.
- o Accept constructive feedback to improve performance without becoming combative or defensive.
- **Self-Regulation**
  - o Remain calm during high-pressure situations and adjust to tight deadlines and conflicts.
  - o Avoid rash decisions that could have long-term impact and take time to evaluate as many perspectives as possible before responding to challenges.
- **Empathy**
  - o Notice when colleagues are struggling and offer your support.
  - o Alter communication to connect with different personalities and cultural backgrounds to ensure inclusive practices and understanding.
- **Social Skills**
  - o Facilitate open dialogue between team members in conflict and lead them to a resolution.
  - o Build strong relationships with peers through effective communication with active listening and mutual respect.
- **Motivation**
  - o Show commitment to your team goals and inspire your colleagues to remain motivated despite challenges and setbacks.

- o Celebrate the success of others on the team and help to foster positive culture and collaboration.
- **Adaptability**
  - o Adjust to changes in the organization with a positive attitude and leading and encourage others to embrace the new opportunities.
  - o Manage unexpected changes and challenges and shifts in work scope and priorities as well as managing potential stressors constructively.
- **Conflict Resolution**
  - o Handle disagreements professionally focusing on solutions and not assigning blame.
  - o Address misunderstandings with open communication to avoid escalation.
- **Leadership**
  - o Provide clear guidance and be approachable and receptive to your colleagues' suggestions.
  - o Recognize and acknowledge team members' contributions, morale, and engagement.
- **Time Management:**
  - o Prioritize tasks and manage workloads efficiently.

Time Management:

Proper time management allows you to do more without the risk of burning out. The key to time management is prioritization – know the difference between "urgent" and "very important" tasks. Prioritizing tasks and managing workloads efficiently is a crucial skill to the workplace.

Individuals who understand how to manage time appropriately avoid distractions, set boundaries, and use productivity tools. Below are some tools for time management.

- **Prioritize Tasks:** Use techniques to focus on tasks and assignments that are urgent and identify the most important task of the day. What needs to be done now? What can be done later? What doesn't need your attention?

- **Use Time-Blocking:** Schedule specific blocks of time for projects and tasks each day. This allows you to get more done within the span of a week. You should also reduce multitasking during blocks of focused work time as this allows you to maximize your blocked time.

- **Set SMART Goals: D**econstruct larger goals into specific steps that make the goal Specific, Measurable, Achievable, Relevant, and Time-bound steps. Breaking down goals makes them more attainable.

- **Minimize Distractions:** Reduce and limit notifications on your devices or implement an app that blocks distractions. Assign designated focus time on your calendar to decrease interruptions and limit notifications on your devices or use apps to block distractions.

- **Leverage Technology:** Use technology to organize and prioritize tasks aligned to deadlines and automate repetitive tasks using software or macros.

- o Examples of software: Asana, Monday.com, and Zoho Projects
- **Practice the Two-Minute Rule:** Complete a task takes less than two minutes, do it immediately instead of adding it to a to-do list.
- **Delegate:** Proper time management doesn't require you to do everything. Managing your time wisely involves delegating. Assign tasks to members of the team and communicate assignment responsibilities.
- **Plan Ahead:** Spend fifteen minutes at the end of the workday in preparation for the next workday or work week by reviewing plans and tasks ahead of time. Planning ahead is a great time management tool for any occasion, especially job readiness.
  - o "If you fail to plan, you are planning to fail," – Benjamin Franklin
  - o Let's take another look at Tyla's interview:

Tyla had been eagerly waiting for an interview opportunity at a marketing agency. She had the qualifications, but when she walked into the interview room, she quickly realized she hadn't prepared as well as she thought. The interviewer asked her about a time she worked with a team and resolved a challenge, and Tyla stumbled, struggling to come up with a clear example on the spot. She also hadn't researched the company thoroughly, so when asked why she wanted to work there, her response lacked depth.

How could Tyla have planned ahead?

    ✓ Research the company
    ✓ Practice common interview questions
    ✓ Mock interviews
    ✓ Organize materials

- **Take Breaks:** Time management is just as much about what you don't do as it is about what you do. Believe it or not, taking a break is also productive! Use techniques that allow you to step away take a break and recharge.
- **Learn When to Say No:** Decline tasks or projects that do not align with your work scope, capacity, or priorities.
- **Reflect and Adjust:** Evaluate and refine your productivity based on what is most effective for you.

Resilience and Grit:

In every workplace, setbacks are inevitable — resilience determines how you bounce back. Maintaining focus and perseverance in the face of setbacks. Grit means sticking to long-term goals even when things get tough. Having both requires perseverance and focus in spite of what might come in the workday.

- **Resilience**
  - **Bouncing Back After Setback:** reflect after a loss of sales, prospect or funding, and adjust

the approach with a focus on a bigger win in the future.

- **Adapting to Change:** adapt to a new system or process that is implemented while maintaining a positive response.

- **Staying Positive Under Pressure:** maintain a positive attitude despite organizational restructuring that may create uncertainty.

- **Handling Criticism Constructively:** receive feedback and improve performance without taking it personally.

- **Overcoming Personal Challenges:** balance work responsibilities with positive outcomes despite personal difficulties they may experience.

- **Grit**
  - **Pursuing Long-Term Goals:** overcome multiple setbacks and remain focused and committed to the vision and mission.

  - **Consistently Meeting Challenge:** remain motivated during a long-term project with significant deadlines, all while maintaining high standards that may be done as a result of personal sacrifices.

  - **Learning and Improvement:** take on difficult tasks or learn new skills to improve their skillset.

- **Taking Initiative:** identify opportunities to improve systems or a process within a company or organization.
- **Dedication to Team Success:** work to support team members during challenging work periods with positive and unwavering commitment to the shared goals of the organization or company.

Before I give you the Power Up move, I want to reiterate that employers are increasingly emphasizing power skills in job postings, performance reviews, and leadership development programs, reflecting their critical role in career success. In reviewing these skills and examples, if there is one area to focus on first, it would be to practice emotional intelligence consistently. This power skill helps to create a more harmonious and resilient workplace culture and environment. Having a clear understanding of these power skills will help you adapt to and become familiar with your work environment, regardless of industry. As a reminder, it is essential to implement these power skills into your workplace behaviors.

POWER UP MOVE
Here's a call to action for you to complete and sharpen your power skills!

1. **Assess:** Which of these skills do you need to improve?
2. **Practice:** Apply these skills in daily work and networking situations.
3. **Grow:** Keep learning, adapting, and refining your power skills.

Chapter 2
Your Digital DNA: Building a Career-Ready Online Presence

"Your digital footprint is like a tattoo - it's permanent, and it tells your story."

Josh's Digital Wake-up Call

Meet Josh, a college freshman majoring in Social Work. He plays soccer, volunteers at a local food pantry, and works part-time at the grocery store. Like many students, Josh was excited to start building a career, hoping to land a meaningful internship at a nonprofit that supports foster care initiatives. With a strong GPA, volunteer experience, and a passion for helping others, Josh felt confident when submitting internship applications.

A few weeks later, Josh received an email from a potential internship supervisor:

"Hi Josh, we appreciate your application and enthusiasm for our program. Before moving forward, we'd like to discuss some concerns regarding your online presence. Let's set up a time to chat."

Confused and slightly panicked, Josh quickly Googled his name. The search results revealed years of old social media posts: some with inappropriate jokes, unfiltered rants about school, and pictures from high school parties. Josh had never considered how these posts might look to a professional organization.

Career preparation includes getting an understanding and awareness of the power of your digital footprint. It consists of preparing yourself to have a strong digital impression that is reflective of who you are in the professional world. Imagine, for just 60 seconds, that you're applying for your dream job or internship? Where is that? Then imagine the hiring manager doing an internet search on your name. What would they find? Would it be a well-rounded, professional social media page displaying your academic achievements and personal goals?

Often, the idea of career-readiness and creating a strong online presence in the digital world can be misaligned, but essentially who you are in your digital footprint will set precedence or preconceived ideas or suggestions. The reality is that more and more companies are looking at online profiles more than personal resumes. In fact, the job-posting website, Indeed, published an article in October 2024, stating that most employers are now doing "social media background checks". Companies are looking to learn more about you, your reputation, your conduct, and your professionalism via your profile page.

I have also spoken to many young career seekers and, often, they think the alternative is that it is better to have no digital presence at all; and that is not the case. It would make logical sense to assume that no social media presence is the safest route; however, it actually does more harm than good. You see, companies actively look for online information on you. And when there is no information to go by, it creates a level of skepticism from the employer. They have nothing that will help them determine who you are, what organizations you've been a part of, what you stand for, why you would be an asset to their company, etc.

In actuality, having a strong, professionally positive presence is important for job seekers. Your digital DNA showcases your professional brand and provides information to potential employers. Oftentimes, potential employers evaluate and review what is presented to evaluate you beyond your resume. Your resume is what you have done and what you're doing, but your online presence shows who you are and allows you to control the narrative. This is an area where I spend a lot of time with young professionals enhancing and developing an online presence that aligns with their skills, talent, and service.

You should also understand that all platforms are not created equal! You should know which platforms you should engage with the most to be able to provide a clear and appropriate digital footprint! And, although they are not all the same, you should also be mindful of the fact that they will all have something to say about you and who you are. For example, you may use a platform like Facebook and LinkedIn to establish a positive digital impression but then use Snapchat and TikTok for fun and personal use. There's nothing wrong with understanding the purpose of each platform, but there is still a level of social responsibility that should be used in every platform. Why? Because they will all be used by companies who want to know the type of person you are. So, be sure to clean up or remove any inappropriate content on social media. A great place to start is by conducting a digital audit!

How exactly does one conduct a digital audit? Utilizing the following steps is an important part of building a positive digital footprint:

- **Audit your digital footprint**:
  - Use any search engine and try to find your online presence. Determine what information about you is publicly accessible. This is a great place to start, and you may be surprised with some of the results.
    - I.E. Open your web browser and search "your name" and the city or state you're from.
    - You can also type in your name and "old social media" in the search bar
    - What did you find?
  - Clean up inappropriate content on social media. Review and delete social media posts, photos, or comments that could be perceived as unprofessional or controversial.
    - Go to your profile and go as far back as when you first joined the social media platform. Click on your old pictures or posts. Ask yourself:
    1. Does this line up with who I am?
    2. Is this what I want potential employers to see?
    3. Could this affect me or others negatively in the long run?

- What about your friends? This is an area most career seekers don't think about. But there's a rather popular expression, *"Tell me who you hang around and I will tell you who you are."* The truth is every social media friend is not necessarily your friend, and every follower is not worth having.

    - Go to your friends and followers list (depending on the platform and profile status) and review each list.

    - Unfollow or unfriend any irrelevant or spammy profiles, or anyone who no longer aligns with your values, beliefs, and ethics

- Set privacy settings, deactivate any unused accounts, and set up alerts for your name to monitor new mentions or content. Everyone doesn't need to tag you on their posts! Make sure it's something you want your name tied to.

- **Build a strong LinkedIn profile**:
    - Why LinkedIn?

        - Imagine a large networking group where you can connect with over 1 billion companies and business professionals in over 200 countries. That is what LinkedIn provides.

        - It is the world's largest professional networking space.

- Use professional photos and share more about who you are. Show viewers what makes you unique and valuable to any organization or company. Lastly, create a compelling summary.

  - Here's an example:

  Passionate About People | Aspiring Social Worker | Seeking Internship Opportunities

  As a dedicated freshman majoring in Social Work at [Your University], I am deeply committed to making a positive impact in communities by advocating for those in need. My passion for helping others has driven me to pursue a career where I can empower individuals, foster meaningful change, and support mental health and well-being.

  Through volunteer work with [Organization Name] and participation in campus advocacy groups, I have developed strong communication, active listening, and problem-solving skills. I am eager to apply these abilities in a hands-on environment where I can learn from experienced professionals while contributing to meaningful social initiatives.

- Showcase your achievements, skills, talent, and volunteerism. Building your career online presence is not just about your career, it's about your make-up. It's about your hobbies, extracurricular activities, values, and passions. You want companies to get to know you as a human being as well.

  - What sports do you participate in? What clubs do you belong to? Volunteer organizations or charity events?

- o Lastly, LinkedIn is extremely educational and informative. Therefore, what you post matters. Use your profile to write longer-form content demonstrating your expertise and knowledge.

- **Leverage social media platforms for professional growth**:
  - o Engage in industry-specific discussions on a variety of platforms where professionals are actively involved in sharing professional content aligned with their specific industry. See some examples below.
    - X (formerly Twitter) is an appropriate platform for technology
    - Instagram is the most (but not the only) appropriate for creatives
    - LinkedIn is widely known and used for business
    - Newer platforms like Blue Sky and Threads are newer and are gaining traction and used for business and technology
  - o Outside of displaying your personality and personal endeavors on your page, you should also create content that speaks to your professional interests. For example, write about a school project you're working on, a lesson you learned at an internship, or articles that you feel add value. See a quick sample post below that can include either an infographic visual to inform or a picture of a

diverse group of children smiling and holding hands.

*Did you know that over **391,000 children** are currently in the U.S. foster care system, with thousands still waiting for a permanent home?* ♥ *Reading this article opened my eyes to the challenges so many children face and the need for more advocacy and support in the system. As a social work student, I'm passionate about finding ways to help families and children in need.*

What are some ways we can support foster youth in our communities? Let's start the conversation! 💬·
#FosterCareAwareness #SocialWork #MakingADifference

- **Showcase achievements and skills:**

    o Use LinkedIn's skills section strategically by listing skills relevant to your desired role and industry.

    o Add certifications, endorsements, and awards to highlight and validate your expertise.

    o Wherever possible, add measurable accomplishments in your work experience section. Connect these measurements to prior work-related experiences and team projects.

Before we get into your Power Up Move, there are a few things I want to emphasize and remind you of. It is very important not to skip these steps in building your digital DNA, as you prepare to launch into career search. Be sure to use your search engine of choice and look for yourself online. What can you find? What might be true? What might be false? Is there anything that you might need to explain to an employer? What alerts should you enable? Remember, your online presence is like a digital imprint, whether you curate it or not, it exists. The real question is whether or not you are shaping it to work in your favor?

In the digital world, no news is NOT good news! Having no online presence at all is like showing up to an interview without a resume. Would you take that risk? Establishing and managing your digital presence is important and takes time that you want to use for a positive outcome. You can enhance your career opportunities as well as establish a positive professional online and in-person profile. Control the social narrative by creating value-add content. Again, I recommend focusing on LinkedIn as well as leveraging other industry-specific platforms. Ultimately, the world needs to see what you bring to the table – which is A LOT! So, highlight your strengths, share your wins, and allow your online presence to reflect your potential!

POWER UP MOVE

Here's a call to action you should do right now! There are a few lines provided below in case you want to write in this book. Scan the QR to connect with Dr. Keisha on LinkedIn.

1. Take 30 minutes to search yourself online and update your online profiles.
2. Write down at least 2 platforms you can leverage for your career.
3. Write a brief LinkedIn summary of yourself.

_____
_____
_____
_____

Keisha Stephenson Taylor, Ed.D.
Nonprofit Leader|College & Career
Readiness Expert|Change Agent|Co...

Chapter 3
Refining Your Career Identity: Craft a Personal Brand and Statement

"What do people say about you when you're not in the room? That's your brand."

Maria's Branding Bust

Maria was a recent college graduate with a degree in Marketing. Like many new graduates, she was eager to land her first job but quickly realized that simply having a degree wasn't enough to stand out in the competitive job market. She sent out dozens of résumés but received very few responses.

Frustrated, Maria turned to a mentor who asked her a simple yet powerful question:
"What makes you different from every other marketing graduate applying for the same roles?"

Maria had never thought about this before. She had strong communication skills, a passion for digital storytelling, and a talent for creating engaging social media content. But none of this was clearly reflected in her résumé, LinkedIn profile, or even how she introduced herself in interviews.

Determined to change her approach, Maria decided to build a personal brand that truly showcased her skills and personality.

Preparing for your career isn't just about sharpening your skills, it also includes creating and maintaining your personal brand. A personal brand makes you unique and unlike any other candidate. Having a personal brand and making it well known will set you apart from your peers. It is oftentimes what gives you a competitive edge. And having a competitive edge in the job market is always a good thing!

Defining Personal Brand
A personal brand is the unique combination of skills, experiences, values, and personality traits that individuals project to the world. This is how you present yourself to a world that doesn't know you. We do this in a variety of ways, and it reflects how a person is known in personal as well as professional settings. A personal brand is crafted and created through activities, communication, style of dress, appearance, and social media presence. Personal Brand can be defined as the reputation you build and evolve over time. What personal brands do for candidates is make a clear distinction of who they are aside from who others are. Your personal brand highlights you and is important because it is how people see you. But, most importantly, it is how they remember you and engage with you personally and professionally.

Think about celebrities or even authors; many of these individuals convey clear and consistent messages which make them unique. They are aligned to the message they want to convey to the world. Each of us has the ability to build and develop a brand. Oprah Winfrey, for example, has built her brand around inspiration, empowerment, and authenticity. Everywhere you look, and everything she is involved in speaks to her brand – from her television show and network to her magazine and philanthropic efforts. This is who she is and everyone knows it, whether she's in the room or not!

Imagine walking into a room full of people, and everyone knows exactly what you stand for—your skills, your values, and what you bring to the table. That's the power of personal branding. The question is, what is your brand saying about you right now, and is it the story you want to tell? Let's start from the beginning with regard to crafting your personal brand.

- **Understand your personal brand**
  - Define your brand identity: before you can build your brand, you need to know what it is as it pertains to you! How do you do that? Ask yourself a few pertinent questions.
    - What are my core values?
    - What am I passionate about?
    - What unique skills or traits do I bring to the table?
    - How do I want others to see me?

In Maria's case, after some reflection, she identified that her core strengths were creativity, digital expertise, and her ability to connect with an audience through storytelling. She is passionate about connecting with people, and she wants people to see and feel that when she's speaking to them.

  - The role of personal branding: a well-defined brand creates opportunities for job offers, networking, and recognition. On the other hand, weak or inconsistent brands can harm credibility and reliability. This is why it's important to define your brand and manage it continuously as this will affect your professional reputation in the future.

- **Steps to build your personal brand**
    o Self-reflection: identify your core values and strengths by homing in on your skills, passions, and values.
    o Here's a quick prompt to help you get started with identifying these things in you:
        "If someone were to describe you in three words, what would you want them to say? Why?
    o Define your unique value proposition: clearly state what sets you apart from others in your respective field. What do you do that others can't or that they might do but not like you?
    o Build an online presence that reflects your brand: how people see you or what they know about you needs to show not just in real life, but also in the virtual world. Therefore, communicating your brand across different platforms like LinkedIn, personal websites, and other social media accounts is crucial to crafting your brand.
        - Let's go back to Maria. After meeting with her mentor, she went back and revamped her LinkedIn profile, started sharing industry-related insights, and even created a personal website to showcase her portfolio.

- Make sure you dive deeper into your online presence in the next chapter!
    o Create consistent messaging: Not only should your online presence reflect your brand, but your resume and bio should also align with your brand messaging. What are you telling the people who see your resume, your social media, etc.? Brand messaging should be clear.
        - Create a well-written professional bio to share when opportunities arise.
        - Use the formula: Who you are + What you do + How you add value = Your brand message.
    o Seek feedback and refine your brand: ask trusted colleagues, family members, and mentors how you come across professionally and personally.

Remember that your personal brand is your professional and personal identity. It's how you present your values, skills, and goals to the world and it's also what sets you apart from the competition. Once you have completed the steps to building your personal brand, you want to think through a statement that reflects your personal brand and unique value.

After you determine your skills, strengths, and values, think about your passions and interests. Take time to think through what makes you unique in your field, what experiences you have had that makes you special in your field. Then, you may also consider creating your **personal brand statement** which is what you want to convey to the world and how you want others to perceive you or your beliefs. Having strong self-awareness strengthens the opportunity to build your brand statement.

- **Crafting your personal brand statement**
    - What is a personal brand statement?
        - The clear and concise declaration of your brand message communicated to the world around you.

As you begin to craft your ideas to develop your statement, you want to think about the target audience. You want to consider the one statement that will be for potential employers or clients, or colleagues. An even bigger audience may be what you want to convey to a professional network. You can always adjust your statement based on your target audience.

- What is the purpose of a personal brand statement?
    - Your personal brand statement is exactly that! It's personal. It's yours and it clearly defines what you stand for in personal and professional spaces.
- Steps to writing a strong brand statement.
    - **Know your audience**: have an awareness of who you are speaking to and adjust your statement accordingly. This could be employers, colleagues, clients, etc.
    - **Be concise and impactful**: try to keep your statement between 3 and 4 sentences but make sure you're intentional about your words so your statement packs a power punch!

- **Use action-oriented language**: what you say and how you say it matters. Demonstrate confidence and clarity when describing your expertise and goals.

As I mentioned above, once you have confirmed who the audience is, you want to begin structuring your statement to be brief, yet bold. You want it to be concise and clear, avoiding words that may be connected to your profession in a way that may not be easily translated or understood. Remember that you have to be mindful of your audience while being true to who you are. You want to describe who you are, what you do, and why you do what you do.

- o Structuring your personal brand statement
  - Start with who you are – your role or industry
  - Highlight what you do best – define key strengths or expertise
  - Explain why it matters – the value you bring
  - Close with your mission or goal – your career vision

People are always looking for others to make a statement that is compelling and impactful. It is important to think about the results you create, and the memories others have shared as a result of your work or time with them.

- o Examples of strong personal brand statements
  - *"I am a digital marketing strategist who helps brands tell compelling stories through content and social media. My passion is creating engaging digital experiences that drive audience engagement and business growth."*

- "*I am a results-driven business leader with a passion for optimizing operations, fostering team growth, and driving sustainable success. With a keen ability to streamline processes and enhance productivity, I specialize in turning challenges into opportunities. My goal is to lead with innovation and integrity, ensuring businesses thrive in a dynamic and ever-evolving marketplace.*"
  - Practice and refine your personal brand statement
    - Your personal brand statement should roll off your tongue naturally. It should feel true to who you are; and, when you practice it and refine it, it does two things. First, it helps you believe it, walk in it and live by it. Second, it provides your audience with a clear picture of you eliminating confusion!

- **Maintaining and evolving your personal brand**
  - Live your brand every day! Your personal brand isn't just what you say, it's also what you do. So, it's important to stay authentic and aligned with your growth – which will be inevitable! When is it appropriate to update your brand?
    - As you gain additional experience in the workplace or with organizations aligned with your goals.
    - If you decide to change career paths or goals.
  - There is power in storytelling in your personal branding

- Personal experiences and stories that align with your brand can also strengthen the authenticity of your brand.

Okay, before we get into the Power Up Move here, let's revisit some points. When working on your personal brand statement, you want to be sure to work with specific details of the actual work or desired work you would like to do. Make sure to reduce assumptions that others can make about your value and be sure to make it memorable. Your personal brand statement is the opportunity to stand out. You want to use your personal knowledge in conveying your message, only you have had the experiences that you want to reference so add that when designing your personal brand statement.

Finally, you want to be sure your message is concise and to the point. You may want to practice writing it out and ensuring you do not exceed three to four sentences. When you practice the statement, if it sounds too long, it probably is. Be sure to revise the statement so that you do not lose the opportunity to deliver your message in a strong statement. The end of your statement should always include your values and intention, these powerful words can leave a lasting impression. Practice your statement in a variety of forums and consider refining as you seek feedback. You want to be as professional and polished as you can, so you want to make time to practice the statement, this way it comes across as authentic and genuine to who you are, and what your message is to the community. You will want to practice and ask a friend, family member, or coach to listen to you and provide feedback.

POWER UP MOVE

Here's a call to action for you to develop your personal brand and craft your brand statement. Feel free to use the lines provided. Don't forget to scan the QR for some more information on developing brand statements.

1. Reflect on what your core values, passions, and unique traits are.
2. Ask 2 friends/family members what 3 words they would use to describe you and why.
3. Write your own four-sentence brand message using the formula: Who you are + What you do + How you add value = Your brand message. Keep it simple.

_____
_____
_____
_____

Chapter 4
Uncover Your Why: Aligning Your Passion, Interests, and Purpose in Your Career

Know yourself. What are you good at, and what do you love to do. These two questions are the building blocks of a fulfilling career.

Sean's Unexpected Encounter with Purpose

Sean always assumed he would follow in his father's footsteps and become an accountant. It was a stable career with great earning potential, and his family fully supported the idea. However, while taking a required business communication class in college, he discovered something unexpected—he had a passion for public speaking and leadership development. Sean found himself excited about presentations, mentoring younger students, and organizing networking events.

Still, he ignored his newfound interest, assuming it was just a hobby. That changed when Sean interned at a corporate firm and realized he felt unfulfilled crunching numbers all day. He admired his manager, who spent time coaching employees, fostering company culture, and helping teams succeed. Sean began to research career options that blended business with leadership and personal development.

Through self-reflection and mentorship, he realized his true passion was in organizational development, helping businesses grow by empowering their people. Sean pivoted, switching his major to Business Administration with a focus on Human Resources. Today, Sean works as a corporate trainer, helping employees build leadership skills and create fulfilling careers.

Career preparation isn't just about skills and education, but it is also about self-discovery. Self-exploration is an extremely significant part of career preparation. Some might think that their career path is pretty straight whether it's because their family members are in the same field or the field offers high-paying positions, or they think a certain industry looks good on paper. Those reasons aren't necessarily wrong, but if your career readiness does not include discovering your passions, interests, and purpose; no career with provide longevity and fulfillment.

Self-exploration in career preparation matters because it offers clarity and direction. When you take time to explore your interests and what "makes drives you", you get a clearer sense of direction. Taking the time to self-discover eliminates the possibility of blindly choosing a career based on external pressures like family expectations or financial prospects. Instead, you are able to make informed decisions that align with your personal values.

On the other hand, not diving into your passions and interests will also cause major implications to your journey in the workplace. Neglecting to discover yourself or depriving yourself of the time to really explore what drives you will lead you on a very long and winding road filled with frustration, confusion, and indecisiveness. I have seen young professionals limit themselves and wear themselves out in the wrong career because they never took a moment to discover what they are passionate about, their interests, and their purpose. Let's take a look at the benefits and drawbacks below.

- **Why self-exploration matters**
    o Gain clarity and direction through self-discovery in order to make informed career choices and eliminate wasting time.
    o Increase job satisfaction and improve engagement, productivity, and motivation by choosing careers that align with personal passions and strengths.
    o Develop a stronger personal brand allowing you to communicate with confidence in different professional settings (see chapter 3).
    o Better adaptability and a strong sense of self-awareness which makes it easier to pivot or adapt to new opportunities.

- **Implications of neglecting self-exploration**
    o Lack of fulfillment and burnout: choosing a career without considering your personal passions and interests can lead to disengagement and emotional exhaustion. How many people do you know who are unhappy in their careers/jobs because they pursued it for reasons other than passion?
    o Frequent career changes: for many reasons, people choose careers that don't suit them which often leads to frequent job-hopping or dissatisfaction. Going from one job to another

repeatedly can make it difficult to build expertise or develop a professional reputation.
- Limited career growth: those who lack an awareness of their passion or purpose may not pursue the right professional development opportunities which makes it difficult to advance. They will either struggle to leverage their strengths or fail to stand out in a competitive job market.
- Missed opportunities: when you don't take the time to reflect on your passions, you run the risk of overlooking non-traditional or emerging career paths that could actually be a perfect fit.

So, what is the best way to think through and discover some of your passions and interests that could also potentially lead you to your purpose? Below, I listed some effective self-exploratory questions that you could ask yourself.

- ❖ What activities make me lose track of time?
- ❖ What problems do I like solving?
- ❖ What skills do I get complimented on often?
- ❖ What workplace values are most important to me?
- ❖ If money wasn't a factor, what would I love to do every day?

Now that we have talked about self-discovery of your passions and interests, let's dive a little deeper into your purpose. While your passions and interests may take you on the career path that is for you, knowing and understanding your "why" will keep you on that path as it grows.

- **Defining your *why***
    - Your *"why"* is your deep-rooted motivation behind your career choice. Often used in the world of entrepreneurship, it is the foundation of your purpose for doing what you do, and it is what will keep you doing it even in challenging situations or seasons of your personal or professional life. Why? Because it fosters a bigger picture!
    - Your *"why"* supersedes money or job titles which are temporary benefits. Rather, its focus is on impact and fulfillment which always lead to long-term gains. More importantly, when you focus on the impact and fulfillment, it almost always leads to those temporary benefits anyway.
    - Sources:
        - Simon Sinek's "Start with Why" Framework
        - Psychology Today on Finding Your Passion

- **Understanding your motivation**
    - What drives you? What makes you feel good about what you're doing? Here, we will briefly discuss a few questions that will help you understand what gets you up in the morning or what drives you to do a certain activity.

- Helping others?
- Creating something new?
- Solving problems?
- Leading and inspiring others?
    o In the case study at the beginning of this chapter, we see how Sean goes from believing that he will be an accountant like his dad to discovering unexpected excitement in presenting, mentoring and helping his peers, and connecting people via organizing events.
    o There are two different types of motivations that I want to share with you here. These are intrinsic and extrinsic motivations.
        - Intrinsic motivations stem from internal satisfaction and enjoyment of doing an activity
        - Extrinsic motivations generate from the receipt of rewards or recognition

- **Identify your strengths and interests**
    o As you take time to self-explore your passions and do some of the activities from earlier in this chapter, you'll be able to zone in on strengths and interests. Some may surprise you, others probably will make complete sense to you. The important thing is that once you can identify them, you can focus on operating in your "zone of genius"!
    o *Zone of genius*: this is a common term used in different professional fields to describe how engaging in activities that utilize our unique

talents, passions, strengths, can cause work to seem effortless while providing a profound sense of fulfillment and joy.
- o How can you identify your strengths and interests? Simple! Practice various forms of assessments.
    - **Self-evaluation:** create a list of different questions for yourself in areas where you excel and things you enjoy doing
    - **Ask your friends/coaches/mentors:** there are things we don't notice about ourselves that others see and it's worth asking them for their viewpoint
    - **Take an online test:** there are various self-assessment tests
    - Take another look at this part of the case study from the beginning of this chapter:

Sean found himself excited about presentations, mentoring younger students, and organizing networking events. Still, he ignored his newfound interest, assuming it was just a hobby. That changed when Sean interned at a corporate firm and realized he felt unfulfilled crunching numbers all day. He admired his manager, who spent time coaching employees, fostering company culture, and helping teams succeed. Sean began to research career options that blended business with leadership and personal development.

Through self-reflection and mentorship, he realized his true passion lay in organizational development—helping businesses grow by empowering their people. Sean pivoted, switching his major to Business Administration with a focus on Human Resources. Today, Sean works as

> *a corporate trainer, helping employees build leadership skills and create fulfilling careers.*

What we don't realize are the steps Sean took after seeing his manager and admiring the work he or she was doing coaching, fostering company culture and helping teams succeed. There are things that Sean did to identify his interests: he researched career options that blended with his particular passions, he self-reflected and got feedback from a mentor.

- **What legacy will you leave?**
  o Everything we've discussed in this chapter is ultimately work you're doing now that will pay dividends later. What do I mean by that? What you're doing now is building a foundation for how you want to be remembered later – your legacy.
  o What do you want to be known for?
  o How do you want to contribute to your community or industry?

Your career choices (no matter what they are) will influence the legacy you leave behind (good or bad). Look at the following examples of how your choices can have both a positive influence on your legacy or a negative influence on your legacy. The first is an example of a good legacy being left behind. The second example is one that will need to be explained for years to come.

Example 1: Bessie Coleman – Launching a Positive Legacy in Aviation

> *Bessie Coleman was the first African American and Native American woman to earn a pilot's license. Denied*

opportunities in the U.S. due to racial and gender barriers, she moved to France to obtain her license in 1921. Coleman used her aviation skills to inspire others, advocating for racial equality and encouraging African Americans to pursue careers in aviation. She performed daring aerial stunts and spoke at schools, leaving behind a legacy that paved the way for future Black pilots, including those in the Tuskegee Airmen. Her determination and passion for flying created a lasting impact in aviation and civil rights.

Key Takeaway: *Bessie Coleman portrays how passion and perseverance can break barriers and create opportunities for others. By staying true to her dreams and using her success to uplift others, Coleman's legacy continues to inspire future generations in aviation and beyond.*

Example 2: Elizabeth Holmes – A Legacy of Scandal and Poor Ethics

Elizabeth Holmes, founder of Theranos, was once hailed as a revolutionary in biotechnology for promising to revolutionize blood testing with minimal samples. However, her company's technology never worked as claimed, and she misled investors, regulators, and the public. The scandal led to her conviction for fraud, demonstrating how ethical failures can overshadow technical ambition. Instead of advancing STEM innovation, Holmes' deception damaged public trust in biotech startups and made investors more skeptical of new health technologies. Her story serves as a cautionary tale about the consequences of prioritizing success over integrity in STEM fields.

Key Takeaway: *Elizabeth Holmes lied to manipulate results in her company. Integrity is essential in career success. No matter how ambitious or groundbreaking an idea may seem, deception and unethical decisions can destroy a legacy and harm an entire industry.*

These two contrasting examples highlight the importance of aligning career choices with ethical values and long-term impact. A positive legacy is built through passion, purpose, and integrity, while poor decisions driven by greed or short-term gains can lead to irreversible consequences. Therefore, determining the type of legacy you want to leave is vital.

- **Research Your Career Interests**
    - When you first start out on this self-exploration journey, the list of career paths might be broad. As you continue to deep dive into your passion, interests, motivations, and your purpose; that may become narrower. Don't hesitate to research different career paths in order to continue on the path that is for you!
    - How do you research careers?
        - Investigate job descriptions that interest you the most
        - Conduct formal interviews with people you may know in the field
        - Seek out opportunities to shadow professionals
        - Get a mentor or network with people who are familiar with the career

So, before we move into your Power Up Move for this chapter, let's recap! Understanding your *"why"* is the foundation of building a fulfilling and impactful career. When you take the time to explore your passions, skills, and interests, you gain clarity on what motivates you and how you can best contribute to the world. As you prepare for the next step in your career journey, self-exploration is key. Ask yourself meaningful questions like what kind of legacy or impact you want to leave. What comes naturally to you and brings you joy? What tasks or activities energize you and make time fly?

By identifying skills and hobbies that feel effortless yet rewarding, you can align your career path with work that not only sustains you but also fulfills you. Researching career fields related to your interests will help you uncover professions that match your strengths and long-term goals. Your career is not just about making a living—it's about making a difference. Take the time to define your why and use it as a guide to shape your future with intention and purpose.

POWER UP MOVE

Here's a call to action for you to start exploring your "why" and defining your legacy. Scan the QR for your free career aptitude test resource!

1. Write down three things you're really good at.
2. Write three activities that make you lose track of time. Use both lists to look for overlaps between them— that's where your passion meets your potential.
3. Write down how you can contribute right now to your community.

Chapter 5
Impact Beyond the Workplace: Building Career Success Through Community Engagement

How Josiah's Community Involvement Led to a Dream Job

Josiah always had a passion for technology and problem-solving. As a college student studying IT, he spent his weekends volunteering at a local nonprofit that provided free coding workshops for underserved youth. At first, it was just a way to give back, but over time, he realized how much he enjoyed teaching and mentoring others.

One day, a guest speaker from a major tech company visited the nonprofit and was impressed by Josiah's ability to break down complex coding concepts for beginners. They exchanged contacts, and a few months later, Josiah was invited to interview for a summer internship. When asked in his interview about leadership and teamwork experience, Josiah highlighted his community work. His ability to apply his skills in a real-world, impactful way set him apart from other candidates.

After completing his internship, Josiah was offered a full-time position at the company. His experience proved that community involvement isn't just about giving back—it's a strategic way to build skills, expand networks, and stand out in a competitive job market.

Becoming active in your community is an effectual part of the career exploration and career development process. You will likely have employers who have companies or organizations which they support and will ask that of their staff and employees as well. What has been interesting as I have worked with young emerging professionals is that they are surprised by this question in the interview process. But if you think about it, it makes complete sense.

Employers are interested in potential employees who have or express demonstrated interest in a community. The term community can be vast. For example, your community can be as unique as supporting an organization like Howling Woods Farm in Jackson Township, NJ which is a sanctuary for surrendered and rescued wolf dogs. It might also consist of supporting an animal shelter or the American Cancer Society. You may build community planting trees, consistently volunteering at your community's food drive, or even teaching classes at your closest community center. Whatever community engagement looks like for you, employers want to know what cause you support that also enhances where you live and work.

As you explore your career and job search, be sure to research the interests and community involvement of the company you are potentially looking to work for. Oftentimes, it is visible on all their platforms. You may be able to see it on their website under community or their social media profiles. In any case, getting involved in your community and with organizations that align with your employer is essential to your career readiness!

So let's delve into community engagement and how you can get involved.

Community Engagement

- **The Role of Community Engagement in Career Development**
    - Employers value community engagement in their candidates because it displays their character, leadership skills, passion and commitment to making positive impact. When it aligns with the company's values, it enhances employee engagement and retention.
    - Active participation in your local community helps sharpen your leadership skills, develop your teamwork abilities, and demonstrates your ability to take initiative – companies love to see those three components.
    - There has been a large increase in trends of companies supporting social responsibility. Check out a few examples of the companies listed below.
        - Microsoft, for example, has committed to becoming **carbon negative by 2030** and aims to remove all the carbon it has emitted since its founding by 2050. The company invests heavily in AI and technology to support global sustainability efforts.
        - Unilever has shifted towards **reducing waste, cutting carbon emissions, and using ethically sourced ingredients** in its products. It has committed to making all plastic packaging **fully recyclable, reusable, or compostable by 2025.**

- Starbucks invests in **ethical coffee sourcing** through its Coffee and Farmer Equity (C.A.F.E.) Practices. It provides free college tuition for U.S. employees through the **Starbucks College Achievement Plan**. The company is working toward a **greener footprint**, aiming for carbon neutrality and waste reduction in stores.

- **How to Identify Where You Can Make an Impact**
    - Before you start getting involved in community work, it's important to have clarity around your personal passions and interests (see Chapter 4). The last thing you want is to get involved in volunteer work you don't enjoy – that will not produce sustainability in your career path.
    - Assess your unique skills and personal strengths that will contribute to producing change in your community. What piece of the puzzle can you bring to the table?
    - Lastly, make sure that your efforts to engage with the community align with your career goals. Everyone should seek to serve but you serve best when you're also doing something that leads you to where you see yourself professionally. Take Josiah's example in the case study above. He was already an IT student and in his spare time, he contributed to his community by teaching coding to underserved youth.

- **Strategies to get involved in your community**
  o Be intentional about where you volunteer and what volunteer activity you're participating in.
    - Search for organizations and volunteer opportunities related to your field
    - If you desire to work in veterinary medicine, you may want to volunteer at a local animal shelter, wildlife rescue center, or pet clinic. Or you could volunteer at a local aquarium.
    - If you want a career in Science Technology Engineering and Math (STEM), you may want to look for local science museums and help out there, or volunteer at elementary school science fairs as a mentor or judge for youth. You can also look for environmental organizations, STEM mentorship programs, and hospitals.
  o Being strategic is about community engagement is just as much about making connections as it is about volunteering. Look to join professional associations in order to expand your network.
    - If you're looking into the sound engineering field, there are several professional associations that will help you expand your network and gain industry insights like the Audio Engineering Society, The Game Audio Network Guild, and the National Association of Music Merchants to name a few.
  o Lastly, consider participating in events that support local and national causes. Take a look at the example on the next page:

> Alex, a college student majoring in biomedical engineering, had a personal connection to diabetes—his younger sister was diagnosed with Type 1 diabetes at the age of seven. Determined to make a difference, Alex sought out ways to engage with his community while gaining hands-on experience in the field of medical research.
>
> He discovered the **American Diabetes Association's Step Out Walk to Stop Diabetes**, a national event raising funds for diabetes research and support services. Wanting to be more than just a participant, Alex volunteered as an event coordinator, organizing fundraising campaigns on his campus. Through this role, he honed skills in event planning, leadership, and communication while networking with healthcare professionals.
>
> Inspired by his experience, Alex took his involvement further by securing a research internship at a local diabetes center. There, he assisted in a study testing new insulin delivery methods, connecting his passion for biomedical innovation with real-world impact.
>
> By the time Alex graduated, his community engagement set him apart from other candidates applying for medical research positions. His initiative not only strengthened his resume but also deepened his commitment to creating life-changing medical advancements.

- **Community connections set you apart professionally**

In all my years of working with employers and young professionals, I can say with assurance that companies are looking for candidates who demonstrate initiative and commitment. Engaging with your community, in whatever capacity works for you, shows that you are not someone who avoids leadership opportunities and supporting the vision and mission of an organization. Getting involved in your community also takes commitment. A position of servanthood cannot be convenient, it must be cause-driven. When you make it about the cause rather than convenience, you stand out to employers.

- o Community involvement helps develop essential workplace skills. If you recall, in chapter one, we thoroughly discussed power skills that are huge factors when interviewing for a position in the job market. Getting involved in your community is a phenomenal way to grow those skills. (See chapter 1).
  - Communication
  - Teamwork
  - Problem-Solving
  - Emotional Intelligence (EQ)
  - Time Management

Aligning your values with companies that prioritize engagement builds a strong professional identity. In chapter 3, we examined the importance of building your career identity which involves your personal and professional brand. When you're looking to volunteer and engage with your community, keep your career identity in mind and make sure whatever you do, it aligns with that.

- **The Power of Mentorship in Career and Community Growth**
  - o Mentoring others strengthens leadership skills.

- Taking on a mentorship role within your community participation enhances leadership skills and shows that you can work with others.
    o Mentoring is a great way to pay it forward!
- You can also help others navigate through their career paths in the same way that someone helped you.

A note about Mentoring

Helping others and mentoring is the gift that keeps on giving. What you put out there undeniably comes back to you. So, as you think about the community and your involvement, think about sharing all that you have learned by bringing others along and sharing what you have learned along this journey.

Engaging with your community is more than just an act of service, it's a key step in career preparation. Volunteering, joining professional associations, and participating in community events allow you to build meaningful connections, develop essential skills, and showcase your commitment to making an impact.

To start, reflect on your interests and passions:

- **What change do you want to see in your community?**
- **Where can your skills contribute to meaningful impact?**
    By answering these questions, you can identify opportunities that align with your values and career aspirations.

Building strong community connections sets you apart by demonstrating qualities that employers value, such as teamwork, leadership, and initiative. It also provides hands-on experience, helps you expand your professional network, and connects you with like-minded individuals and organizations that prioritize community involvement.

Your career is not just about what you do, it's about the impact you make. Whether it's mentoring, advocating for a cause, or supporting initiatives that matter to you, community engagement strengthens both your personal and professional growth. As you move forward in your career journey, consider how your contributions can leave a lasting impression on the world around you.

POWER UP MOVE
Here's a call to action for you to get started engaging with community. Scan the QR for additional resources!

1. Pick 3-4 different companies in the industry of your choice and research what nonprofit organizations they partner with or causes they participate in.
2. Research 3 community organizations or activities that are aligned with your values and career interests.
3. If you're not already, sign up to get involved with a local community event or initiative.

Chapter 6
Stepping into Opportunity: Maximizing Career Fairs for Success

Malachi Turned a Career Fair into a Job Offer

Malachi, a recent college graduate passionate about marketing, was unsure about how to break into the field. After learning about an upcoming career fair on campus, Malachi took the time to research attending companies, identifying a few that aligned with his interests.

Before the fair, he refined his elevator pitch and printed multiple copies of his resume. On the day of the event, he dressed professionally and approached recruiters with confidence. One company, a growing digital marketing agency, was particularly impressed with his enthusiasm and portfolio.

Following the event, Malachi took the extra step to send personalized thank-you emails to the recruiters he met. A week later, he received an invitation for an official interview, leading to his first full-time job in digital marketing.

Here is another example for high school students:

Jasmine's Apprenticeship Journey

Jasmine, a high school junior with a curiosity for technology and design, had always been the student who enjoyed tinkering with gadgets and helping her classmates troubleshoot computer issues. When her school counselor announced an upcoming apprenticeship opportunity with a local tech firm, Jasmine hesitated—she wasn't sure she had enough experience. But with encouragement from a teacher, she applied and was accepted into the program.

The apprenticeship placed Jasmine in the IT department of a growing startup, where she shadowed tech professionals, learned basic coding, and even assisted with hardware setups. Jasmine treated the experience like a real job—she showed up early, asked questions, and kept a journal of everything she learned. Her mentors noticed her enthusiasm and professionalism, often commenting on her positive attitude and willingness to learn.

By the end of the semester, Jasmine not only gained hands-on experience and a clearer idea of her future path, but she also earned a glowing letter of recommendation and was offered a paid summer internship. The experience gave her a head start on her future and helped her feel more confident about exploring a tech-related career after graduation.

Imagine going on a trip to shop for fruit for a special dessert you're making. You walk into a farmer's market on a Saturday morning because you know there is a fruit stand that will have exactly what you're looking for. Every booth represents something unique—fresh produce, handmade goods, locally brewed coffee—but you are specifically looking for fruit for your dessert. You know the fruit that you need, and you look for stands that offer it. Each vendor has their line of produce and is hoping to connect with people who value what they offer. Now picture yourself walking through the rows: asking questions, tasting samples, comparing options, and maybe even finding your new favorite fruit stand.

That's exactly what attending a career fair is like.

Clearly, we're not talking about fruit stands and farmer's markets, but career fairs are a good place to source opportunities and to practice your interviewing skills. You may find opportunities online or from other sources, and if there are companies that will be present, there is preparation that must take place. Oftentimes there are hiring fairs in the community as well as on college campuses.

Take a look at the following key points about college fairs and the steps to prepare beforehand.

- **Why Career Fairs Matter**
  - Like going to a car dealership where you know you can view all your car-buying options, attending career fairs gives you direct access to recruiters and hiring managers.
  - At the car dealership, you have the opportunity to see all different models, colors, and types of vehicles. Likewise, career fairs offer the opportunity to explore different industries and job roles.
  - Like test driving a car, career fairs also provide you with the chance to practice networking and interviewing in a low stake's environment.

- **Preparation is key!**
  - Preparing for a career fair is the same whether it's in person or online (virtually)

Liza's Game Plan for Career Fair Day

Liza is a college senior majoring in Communications with a passion for media and public relations. She recently learned about an upcoming career fair happening on her campus and saw that several major media companies, local PR firms, and nonprofit organizations would be in attendance.

Determined to make a great impression, Liza put together a game plan:

- **Before the Fair:**
  Liza started by reviewing the list of participating companies. She circled five that matched his interests and spent time researching each one—checking out recent press releases, learning about their work culture, and even looking up job openings they had posted online. She wrote down thoughtful, tailored questions to ask the recruiters so she wouldn't be caught off guard. She also updated her resume, had it reviewed by her career counselor, and printed out 15 clean copies. She even ordered simple business cards with her contact information and LinkedIn profile to leave a lasting impression.

- **During the Fair:**
  Liza dressed professionally in business casual attire that reflected both polish and her personality. As she approached each booth, she confidently introduced herself and delivered a well-practiced elevator pitch that highlighted her background, interests, and what kind of role she was seeking. Liza made sure to shake hands, ask questions, and jot down notes after each

conversation—especially the names of recruiters and anything specific they mentioned about next steps.

- **After the Fair:**
  That evening, Liza sent personalized thank-you emails to the recruiters she spoke with, referencing parts of their conversation and reiterating her enthusiasm. One recruiter from a PR agency responded the next day, inviting her to a follow-up interview the following week.
    o Let's take Liza's example above and extract the key steps to preparing for a career fair.
        - Research the companies that will be attending.
        - Develop a tailored list of questions for recruiters.
        - Prepare and print updated resumes, and if applicable, business cards.
        - Plan your outfit based on the event's level of formality.

- **Make a strong first impression**
    o As beneficial as attending career fairs can be, it can also set you up for success or leave you out to dry. You see, during the course of a fair, you only have a certain amount of time to make a strong first impression. You have a few minutes in conversation to stand out, which is why you have to make every minute count.
    o Since time is limited at career fairs, let me give you a few tips for making a strong first impression.

- Practice your elevator speech: this is your 30-second introduction highlighting your skills, experience, and career goals.
- Maintain eye contact, give an assertive handshake, and demonstrate confidence in conversation.
- Record any notes on the companies you meet with and details about the ones that interest you the most.

- **The fortune is in the follow-up!**
  - Once the career fair is over, you're not quite done yet. You have one more extremely important step that will, again, set you apart and make your interaction memorable. Follow up!
  - Here are a few tips for following up after the career fair:
    - Send thank-you emails to recruiters or professionals with whom you connected.
    - Reinforce interest by referencing specific details from your conversation.
    - Connect on LinkedIn to continue building relationships.

To wrap up this chapter, let's review. Career fairs are more than just events—they're launching pads for opportunity. Whether you're attending virtually or in person, how you prepare and present yourself can make a lasting impression on potential employers. This chapter walked you through the steps to confidently approach these events and take full advantage of what they offer.

Earlier I gave you a few "career fair hacks". Here they are again. Before the fair, it's crucial to do your homework. Researching the companies attending helps you tailor your questions and stand out as a well-informed candidate. Bring multiple copies of your updated resume, and if possible, have professional business cards on hand to leave a quick and easy way for recruiters to remember you.

During the fair, presentation is everything. Dress professionally in a way that aligns with the industry you're pursuing. Be prepared to introduce yourself with a brief, polished elevator pitch that communicates who you are, what you're looking for, and what you bring to the table. As you speak with recruiters, take notes about who you meet and what is shared—these details will come in handy for thoughtful follow-ups.

Lastly, always ask questions about the next steps in the hiring process, including what attire or materials might be appropriate for future interviews or networking opportunities. Career fairs can feel overwhelming, but with the right preparation and mindset, they become a valuable step in building your professional future.

POWER UP MOVE

Here's a call to action on how to search, attend, and leverage career fairs. Don't forget to scan the QR for some more information on career fairs!

1. Research and save the date of at least 2 career fairs for you to attend
2. Write a list of questions you'd want to ask the recruiters of the companies of your choice if you met them at a career fair.
3. Practice your 30-second elevator speech.

Chapter 7
Purpose Evolution – Building the Skills that Build Your Future

Kenya's Internship Turnaround

Kenya, a college sophomore, landed a competitive internship at a local marketing agency. Excited but unprepared for the fast-paced environment, she quickly found herself overwhelmed—missing deadlines and showing up late. After a crucial check-in with her supervisor, who emphasized the importance of professionalism and time management, Kenya took initiative. She created a detailed planner, blocked time off for tasks, and started arriving 15 minutes early. By the end of the internship, her transformation was evident. Her team praised her growth, and she was offered a part-time role during the school year—with the potential for full-time placement after graduation. Kenya's story illustrates the power of developing soft skills and taking ownership of your growth.

As you step into new seasons of life; whether it's starting college, finishing your degree, or launching your career, there are three powerful tools that will help you stand out: professionalism, career development, self-development. These aren't just buzzwords—they're game changers. Let me explain why. Professionalism helps you build trust, show up with integrity, and follow through on your commitments. A trait that will not only set you apart in the job market, but will also shape how effectively you perform, collaborate with others and lead over time.

Career development is all about planning your future, making connections, and taking steps to reach your goals. And self-development? That's how you grow—by learning, adapting, and becoming the best version of yourself. In a world that's always changing, these skills give you the confidence and direction to succeed, not just today, but for the long haul. This chapter explores why these skills matter now more than ever—and how intentionally developing them can lead to lasting success in college, career, and life.

Professionalism:

- **What is professionalism and why does it matter?**
    - Professionalism is a combination of how you conduct yourself, behavior, attitude, competence, respect, and commitment to performing in excellence.
    - In a student setting, you can demonstrate professionalism by being punctual to class or professional functions, being prepared, interacting respectfully with others, communicating effectively, committing to your learning, and accepting accountability openly.
    - Focusing on these will help you enhance your professional skills once you transition into a work setting.

- **How professionalism shapes perception**

- There are several ways in which professionalism shapes how others view you and your ethics. Here are a few examples:
  - **Punctuality shows respect and consideration.** When you show up on time, you are sending a message that you care about someone else's time, and you take your commitments seriously. Whether it's a class, a work shift, a meeting or an interview; when you arrive on time, the impression others get is that you are organized, dependable, and responsible.
  - **Reliability builds trust.** Trust in the workplace is not a quick thing to obtain, it must be earned. However, showing others that they can count on you to follow through provides a level of trust that only grows each time you demonstrate reliability. Whether it's completing a group project or showing up for an event, when you're seen as a dependable person, people want to work with you.
  - **Clear communication forges strong connections.** We've all heard the expression, "Choose your words wisely." Well, I say we should choose how we say them wisely as well. The way you communicate (speak, write, and listen) all contributes to how you are perceived by those around you. When you communicate and interact effectively (respectfully and thoughtfully), you build

credibility and show emotional intelligence.

Some may question the opportunity to demonstrate professionalism at a part-time job. Does it really matter? Will it make a difference? Especially if you're temporarily working in a part-time position that isn't lined up with your desired industry. The answer is absolutely! At the very least, for matters of integrity. But also because it says something about YOU and speaks to your legacy. Take a look at the example below:

Tommy, a sophomore in college, worked part-time as a front desk assistant at a local gym. From the very beginning, he made it a point to arrive a few minutes early for each shift, dressed neatly, and greeted every member with a warm and professional attitude. When the gym's manager needed someone to cover a shift on short notice, he consistently stepped up without complaint.

Tommy also took the initiative to reorganize the check-in process making it more efficient, which didn't go unnoticed. His reliability, respectful communication, and consistent work ethic stood out so much that, by the end of the semester, he was offered a promotion to shift supervisor and a glowing letter of recommendation securing an internship for Tommy in a completely different field – aviation – proving that professionalism transcends industries and opens doors you might not expect.

Building Career Habits:

- It is never too early to start building good career habits. There are several ways to get prepared now.
    o Goal setting: setting goals is a great habit to start forming early in your career-seeking path.
    o Resume-building: practice building your resume early as this will help you add on to it as you engage in your community, start working, and move up academically.
    o Informational interviews: these are conversations with professionals working in fields or roles that interest you, designed to gather information rather than secure a job.
- It's never too late to build an online presence.
    o LinkedIn, Alignable (refer to Chapter 2)
- While it's beneficial to start good career habits, it's also important to understand that career development is not a one-time event. It's an ongoing, lifelong process. So you should never stop building your career habits.

Self-development:

- There is power in self-development and candidates who understand that establish their identities, early on, as "lifelong learners".
- A lifelong learner is someone who proactively and continuously looks to obtain new knowledge, build new skills, and create new experiences – going above and beyond formal education. They are always curious and ask questions to feed their

curiosity. No learning is beneath them as they see it all for good use.
- Developing "self" also requires a heightened level of self-awareness, adaptability and skill building which will keep you relevant in the long run.
    - Self-awareness – you are constantly checking in with yourself, your skills, your capacity, and your abilities; understanding where you are helps you identify what you need for where you're going.
    - Adaptability – you're in tune with the environment and you operate with flexibility that ultimately helps the organization.
    - Skill-building – you continually look for opportunities and ways to build, sharpen, and expand your skillset which opens the door for greater possibilities in your field.
- Self-development best practices
    - Take free online courses like Udemy, Coursera, FutureLearn, or Codecademy (to name a few).
    - Read relevant articles pertaining to your industry.
    - Look for mentorship within your industry or via networking.

Professionalism, Career-building, and Self-development:

As you prepare to graduate high school, navigate college, or take your first steps into the working world (whichever pertains to you), understanding how professionalism, career development, and self-development work together can give you a significant edge. These aren't just individual skills to check off a list, they are interconnected habits that, when practiced together, help shape your character, confidence, and career readiness.

Professionalism is more than how you dress or speak (although that matters as well), it's about being dependable, respectful, and showing up as your best self, even when no one is watching. Career development builds on this by pushing you to take ownership of your future, whether that means exploring your interests, setting goals, or learning how to network effectively. At the same time, self-development is what fuels your personal growth – it's the inner work that helps you adapt, overcome challenges, and stay sharp in a world that's always changing.

To make these habits a part of your daily routine, start small. Maybe that means creating a study schedule and sticking to it, reaching out to a mentor for advice, or joining a student organization that aligns with your interests. Set weekly or monthly goals, track your progress, and celebrate your wins along the way. These seemingly simple actions build a foundation for lifelong success.

Here are a few journal prompts to help you reflect and grow:

- **Where in my life can I improve my professional presence?**
- **What's one career development goal I can set for the next 3 months?**

- **What's a skill I need to strengthen, and how can I start today?**

Intentionally weaving professionalism, career planning, and self-growth into your journey now means you'll be setting yourself apart – not just as a student, but as a future leader.

Here's what is crucial to understand, as you step into different positions (i.e. internships, part-time roles, or your first full-time job), it's important to understand what employers are truly evaluating beyond just your resume. In fact, some don't even consider resumes as a primary source of candidate information. Truthfully, from the moment you apply, employers are assessing your professionalism, your dedication to personal growth, and your readiness to take ownership of your career. They're not just hiring for skills they're hiring for mindset, work ethic, and potential.

Employers look for individuals who can work independently but also thrive in teams. They value candidates who show initiative, seek feedback, and are committed to continuous improvement. Whether it's showing up on time, communicating clearly, or investing in your own development, these small behaviors signal that you're someone who takes their future seriously.

When you combine professionalism, career development, and self-development, you present yourself as someone who's not only ready for the job—but someone who's ready to grow with the organization. That's the kind of candidate who stands out in a competitive job market and builds a lasting career.

POWER UP MOVE

Here's a call to action on building skills that will help evolve your purpose. Scan the QR for more information on how to elevate your career prep game!

1. Think about your school, part-time job, or volunteer role (or even at home); how do you demonstrate professionalism based on what is stated in this chapter?
2. What areas of professionalism and/or self-development do you need to focus on?
3. Choose one of the self-development best practices and complete it today. What did you find?

Chapter 8
Staying on Track: Building a Career That Grows with You

How Malik Unleashed Momentum

Malik, a recent high school graduate, wasn't sure what career he wanted to pursue. He knew he liked technology and problem-solving, so he enrolled in an entry-level IT course while working part-time at a retail store. Over the next year, Malik continued to build on his interest by taking free online certifications and volunteering to help a local nonprofit with its digital tools. He also created a LinkedIn profile, reached out to mentors, and attended two community career fairs.

By the time he applied for an apprenticeship at a local tech company, Malik already had a basic resume, practical experience, and a digital network. Not only did he land the apprenticeship, but his strong work ethic and proactive learning mindset earned him a full-time position within the year. His journey shows how staying on track and investing in your growth can pay off—no matter where you start.

No matter where you are in your journey, be that fresh out of high school, halfway through college, or navigating life after graduation, staying on track in your career development is both a mindset and a strategy. The road to a fulfilling and sustainable career isn't always a straight line, sometimes there are curves that come with it.

However, with the right tools and intentional steps, you can continue moving forward with clarity and confidence.

In my line of work, I've found that today's job market is dynamic, fast paced, and often unpredictable. That's why it's more important than ever to not only explore what you want to do, but also to build a toolkit of skills and habits that keep you prepared for whatever comes next. Staying on course so that you can continuously build in your career is essential. This chapter is your career compass—it's packed with actionable strategies and a checklist you can refer back to as you grow.

In these next few pages, we'll discuss how to gain relevant skills, build a strong personal brand, network intentionally, and stay flexible in a changing world. Whether you're aiming for college, the workforce, a trade program, or an entrepreneurial path, the steps you take now can shape the opportunities you step into later.

This isn't just about landing your first job, it's about building a career that evolves with you. Let's dive into how you can stay the course and create a professional life that reflects your values, strengths, and potential.

- **Self-Discovery & Goal setting**
    - We touched on self-discovery in chapter 4; and, in the last chapter, we also discussed goal setting. However, here I will emphasize the importance of identifying these two areas as they pertain to you in order to continue enhancing your career path.
    - Because you are taking the time to uncover your strengths, interests, and values early on,

you have the advantage of being able to fortify these three and grow them as you continue the path you're on. You should keep working on these attributes even as you're in the world of work because it will help you identify your next steps as you progress.
- Although we did talk about goal setting, I want to go a little more in depth here as you keep moving in your career path. Continuously setting long-term and short-term goals keeps you focused.
- What do short-term and long-term goals look like? And how do you set them? Check out a few examples and tips below.
  - 6-month goals: this short-term goal setting may look something like: establishing a solid and consistent online presence, attending a certain number of career fairs, building a resume draft, etc.
  - 1-year goals: this short-term goal setting may look like: volunteering at a community center or organization, working at an internship of your choice, etc.
  - 5-year goals: this long-term goal setting may look like: securing the position you want, applying for a promotion within your company, moving into another area within the industry of your choice, etc.
  - Here are some questions to ask yourself when you're setting short-term and long-term goals:
    - *What do I want to achieve and by when?*
    - *Where do I see myself in 6 months? In 1 year? In 5 years?*

- *Is where I want to go realistic for where I am today?*
- *What would I need to do today to get there?*
  - Another helpful way to enhance self-discovery and goal setting is by utilizing tools like personality assessments and career quizzes. Check the QR code in chapter 4 for resources.

- **Skill-building and gaining experience**
  - Foundationally, the best way to build your skills and gain experience is through part-time jobs, volunteer work, internships, and online courses.
    - These all give you a taste of what the world of work has to offer.
    - These environments provide additional opportunities to learn and sharpen the power skills we discussed in chapter 1.
  - Soft skills vs. Hard skills – understanding they both add value to the workplace
    - Soft skills are personal attributes, traits, and social cues that are essential for navigating the workplace and interacting with others in a work environment.
      - Communication
      - Teamwork
      - Adaptability
      - Problem-solving
      - Critical thinking
    - Hard skills are specific skills and knowledge that are acquired through education, training,

and experience; and they are essential to completing a specific task.
- Software proficiency
- Technical skills
- Job-specific functions

- **Resume & job application readiness**
  - It's perfectly okay if your resume isn't filled with years of work experience just yet but you should definitely still have one. Rather than a list of jobs, you can focus on potential, transferable skills, and effort. Here are a few examples of what you can include on your resume to start:
    - Education: Include your current school, graduation date, GPA (if above 3.0), and any relevant coursework or academic achievements.

      Example:
      Springfield High School, Springfield, IL
      Expected Graduation: May 2025
      GPA: 3.7 | Honor Roll | AP Biology, Intro to Business, Dual Credit English

    - Volunteer experience: Highlight service work, community involvement, or school-organized service projects. These show responsibility, commitment, and initiative.

      Example:
      Volunteer – Local Animal Shelter
      June 2023 – Present
      • Assisted with daily care of animals and front desk support
      • Communicated with visitors and helped with adoption events

- Extracurricular activities & leadership: Clubs, sports, student government, or campus involvement show teamwork, leadership, and dedication.

  Example:
  Treasurer – Student Council
  • *Managed budget for school events and fundraisers*
  • *Collaborated with council members to organize Spirit Week*

  Member – STEM Club
  • *Participated in robotics competitions and science fairs*

- Part-time or seasonal job: Even a few hours a week counts. Focus on responsibilities and what you learned.

  Example:
  Cashier – Target
  August 2022 – Present
  • *Provided excellent customer service and handled transactions*
  • *Trained new hires on POS system and store procedures*

- Skills: Include both hard and soft skills (just make sure you can back them up if asked!).

  Example:
  Microsoft Office & Google Workspace
  Canva & basic video editing
  Time Management
  Customer Service

- Awards & Certifications: Include anything from academic honors to certifications.

- Additionally, your cover letters matter just as much as the resumes! It is especially important to make sure your resume and your cover letters are tailored to specific jobs. Regarding your cover letter, make sure you do not use a generic one for every company. Instead, create one that can be edited to speak to the company you're sending it to.
- That makes a personal connection to the hiring manager. Be mindful of words and phrases that can be detected that may negatively impact the review of the letter and resume. Often times, the resume and letter are reviewed by an AI tool first before it gets to the hiring manager
- Lastly, tap into the resources and feedback from mentors and career services at your school.

- **Long-lasting networking and professional relationships**
  - **Here are tips for attending in-person events:**
  - Attend events with intention: Go to career fairs, club meetings, community workshops, or speaker events. Create a list of who you'd like to meet or what industry you'd like to connect with. Come prepared with questions and goals for what you want to learn from who you want to meet.
  - Perfect your elevator pitch: I already talked about the importance of being ready to share a 30–60 second introduction that includes your name, what you're studying or interested in, and what you're hoping to do.

- Be curious and ask questions: People love to share their stories. Ask about their career paths, current roles, or what advice they'd give to someone starting out.
- Follow up: After meeting someone, send a quick thank-you message via email or LinkedIn. Mention something specific you talked about to jog their memory and keep the relationship going.

- **Here are a few tips for attending online events:**
- Have a strong LinkedIn profile
- Connect with intention: end connection requests to classmates, professors, people you meet at events, and professionals in your field. Always include a short message when sending a request:
- Engage with online content
- Use alumni networks: Many colleges and high schools have alumni groups on LinkedIn or Facebook. Reach out to graduates in your field of interest; most are happy to offer advice or a referral.

BONUS TIP: Be Yourself and be consistent. Networking isn't about being perfect—it's about being **genuine** and **open to learning**. Over time, consistent engagement (asking questions, offering help, staying in touch) builds a strong network that supports your growth.

- **Job search and interview prep**
  - A great way to launch your job search process is to research job roles that align with your

values and skillset. Let me give you a few ways to do that.
- Utilize career assessment tools that help identify your strengths, interests, and values to match them to potential careers, i.e. CareerOneStop
- Browse through online platforms like LinkedIn, Indeed, or Handshake to explore job descriptions. Specifically look at required skills, company mission and values, and teams that are involved in that job.
- Reach out to mentors or professionals in your field of interest and conduct informational interviews. Ask them questions like what their typical day looks like or what they love most about their career.
- Visit company websites to see if their culture and values align with yours. Check their mission/vision statements, social responsibilities, etc.
- Reflect on your own past experiences to identify what school projects or jobs gave you the most fulfillment, where you felt the most energized, and what causes or community activities you care about most.

o No one should ever assume to walk into an interview with a resume and simply answer questions. Preparation takes the overwhelm out of having to constantly think on the spot. Not that there won't be any questions where you'll have to, but practicing minimizes the chances of your mind going blank.
- Prepare and write down questions (based on your character and what you know about the company) that you believe could be asked in an interview.
- Just like you did for informational interviews, reach out to a mentor or professional in your

field of interest to ask what questions they believe you would be asked in an interview. Or, if you have a relationship with that person, ask if they would role play and conduct a practice interview with you.
- o Keep the job search process going! Regardless of where you are in this path, be it looking for a part-time job or working in an internship or starting your new full-time job; make these steps a best practice whenever you're ready to move in your career path.

Lastly, I want to briefly hit on personal branding and professionalism which has been discussed in depth throughout this book. In today's world, your personal brand begins long before you step into a job interview, it starts online. And we talked a lot about what that looks like, so I just want to reiterate the fact that employers often search for candidates' social media profiles to get a glimpse into their personality, professionalism, and judgment. This means your digital presence is no longer just "personal," it's part of your public reputation. At the beginning of this book, I mentioned that high school and college students alike should take time to clean up their social media accounts, remove unprofessional content, and build a more polished, intentional presence that aligns with the careers they want to pursue. This is a topic I'm extremely passionate about because I've seen and participated in calls with companies that are adamant about tapping into online platforms to determine a candidate's character, reputation, and compatibility – not just their resume.

Your personal brand also includes how you present yourself in real life—your appearance, reliability, attitude, and communication style all help shape how others perceive you. So it is crucial for you to understand that these companies are watching you. They want to perceive if you are consistent, respectful, and dependable. These small yet powerful traits leave lasting impressions on professors, employers, and peers. Professionalism isn't about perfection—it's about being responsible, accountable, and ready to rise to the occasion with integrity.

In addition to seeing who you are at your core, they want to know what you can do – your bandwidth. The job market is constantly shifting; new tools, technologies, and career paths emerge all the time. That's why adaptability and a mindset for continuous learning are essential skills for long-term success. Whether you're exploring trade careers, STEM fields, creative industries, or business, one thing remains true: those who are willing to learn and grow will stand out.

Growth opportunities come in many forms; taking online courses, joining a student organization, stepping into a leadership role, attending a workshop, or pursuing a certification. These steps don't just add to your resume; they build your confidence, expand your skill set, and show initiative. Lifelong learners are more resilient, more capable of navigating career shifts, and more likely to thrive in an ever-changing workforce.

Summary and Closing Thoughts:

This final chapter has equipped you with practical tools to stay on track in your career development journey. From discovering your strengths, forging essential skills, and setting meaningful goals, to building real-world experience and crafting a strong personal brand—each section has been designed to help you move forward with clarity and confidence.

You've learned how to create resumes that reflect your growth, how to network both online and in-person, and how to align your job search with your personal values and skills. You've also explored the importance of professionalism—how you show up, communicate, and present yourself matters more than you may think. And perhaps most importantly, you've been encouraged to embrace a mindset of continuous learning and adaptability, traits that will serve you well in every stage of life. Let me give you a few final thoughts about your path…

1. Your path doesn't have to be perfect to be powerful.
Early in your career, it's easy to think you have to "figure it all out." But the truth is, your journey will evolve. Be open to change, and let your interests and passions guide you over time.

2. Take initiative – even if you're unsure.
Don't wait until you have all the answers. Volunteer for projects, speak up in meetings, and pursue stretch opportunities. Growth comes when you step just outside your comfort zone.

3. Find mentors – and be a great mentee.
Surround yourself with people who challenge and support you. Ask questions, stay open to feedback, and remember that mentorship is a two-way street.

4. Focus on learning, not just titles.
This is the time to build skills, explore industries, and understand what lights you up. The experience you gain now will serve you, even if you pivot later.

5. Set boundaries and protect your energy.
Ambition is great, but burnout is real. Learn to prioritize, say no when needed, and create habits that support your well-being.

6. Keep showing up—and trust the process.
There will be hard days. Imposter syndrome. Rejections. Confusion. Keep showing up anyway. Progress often looks like small wins stacked over time.

Special note to High School Seniors

Having gone through this book, I want you to feel that you have a head start on your career path. I have a few tips I want to leave specifically for you.

1. It's okay not to have it all figured out.
You're still discovering who you are and what you want – *and that's exactly where you're supposed to be*. Give yourself permission to explore.

2. Every experience counts.
That part-time job, volunteer gig, or group project? It's teaching you something. Show up with purpose and treat every opportunity like a steppingstone.

3. Don't let fear stop you.
Apply for the scholarship. Audition for the role. Introduce yourself to that speaker. Confidence isn't about never being afraid—it's about doing it anyway.

4. Ask questions and stay curious.
Curiosity leads to clarity. The more you learn, the more you'll uncover what excites you and what doesn't. That's how you find your path.

5. Your journey is your own.
It might take longer. It might look different. It's still *valid*. Don't compare – just commit to moving forward.

6. Your story matters.
Where you come from, what you've been through – it all adds value. Use your voice. Be proud of your roots. You belong in every room you step into.

POWER UP MOVE
Here's a call to action for you! Don't forget to scan the QR for some more information on fueling your future in your ongoing career journey.

1. Based on where you are, set your 6-month, 1-year and 5-year goals. (You can always adjust them).
2. Using the information above, list a few things you can include to start building your own resume.
3. Pick three points under Job search and Interview prep that you can complete within the next 2 weeks.

As this book comes to a close, remember: **your career path is not a straight line—it's a journey of self-discovery, trial and error, growth, and perseverance.** Whether you're a high school senior, a college student, or a recent graduate, you already have what it takes to build a purposeful and impactful future.

Keep showing up. Keep asking questions. Keep building the skills that matter.

This isn't the end—it's your launching point.
Fuel your future with intention, and there's no limit to where you can go!

Career Prep Checklist

✓ **1. Self-Discovery & Goal Setting**

☐ Identify personal strengths, skills, and interests

☐ Explore different career paths and industries

☐ Set short-term (6 months–1 year) and long-term (3–5 years) career goals

☐ Research potential career paths and industries

✓ **2. Building Skills & Experience**

☐ Gain work experience through internships, apprenticeships, or part-time jobs

☐ Learn new skills through online courses, workshops, or trade schools

☐ Develop essential soft skills (communication, teamwork, problem-solving)

✓ **3. Resume, Cover Letter, or Job Application Readiness**

☐ Write a basic cover letter that highlights your skills and motivation

☐ Gather references from past employers, teachers, or mentors

☐ Create or update your resume with relevant experiences

- Write a professional cover letter tailored to job applications
- Have a mentor or career advisor review your resume

✓ **4. Networking & Professional Connections**

- Build connections with professionals in fields of interest
- Attend job fairs, community events, or industry workshops
- Develop an elevator pitch for networking conversations
- Seek a mentor or career coach for guidance

✓ **5. Job Search & Interview Preparation**

- Research job opportunities in industries that align with career goals
- Apply to multiple jobs using tailored resumes and applications
- Practice interview questions and professional communication skills
- Follow up after interviews with a thank-you message

✓ **6. Professionalism & Personal Branding**

- Maintain a professional image online (clean up social media profiles)
- Create a LinkedIn profile or digital portfolio (if relevant)

- Develop a strong work ethic, reliability, and professionalism

✓ **7. Continuous Learning & Growth**

- Stay informed about industry trends and job market changes
- Take on leadership roles in community or workplace settings
- Maintain a professional online presence (clean up social media)
- Join professional organizations or student career clubs
- Seek feedback and continue learning new skills

www.ingramcontent.com/pod-product-compliance
Lightning Source LLC
Chambersburg PA
CBHW050915160426
43194CB00011B/2419